SPACE ROBOTS

LUKE COLINS

Bolt Jr. is published by Black Rabbit Books
P.O. Box 3263, Mankato, Minnesota, 56002.
www.blackrabbitbooks.com

Grant Gould, designer; Omay Ayres, photo researcher

Names: Colins, Luke, author.
Title: Space robots / by Luke Colins.
Description: Mankato, Minnesota : Black Rabbit Books, [2020] | Series: Bolt Jr. World of robots | Includes bibliographical references and index. | Audience: Age 6-8. | Audience: Grades K to 3. | Identifiers: LCCN 2019003844 (print) | LCCN 2019004881 (ebook) | ISBN 9781623101725 (e-book) | ISBN 9781623101664 (library binding) | ISBN 9781644661109 (paperback)
Subjects: LCSH: Space robotics—Juvenile literature.
Classification: LCC TL1097 (ebook) | LCC TL1097 .C65 2020 (print) | DDC 629.8/920919–dc23
LC record available at https://lccn.loc.gov/2019003844

Printed in the United States. 5/19

Image Credits

jpl.nasa.gov: NASA/Jet Propulsion Laboratory, 6–7, 16–17; mars.nasa.gov: NASA, 8–9; NASA/InSight Mission, 5, 18; nasa.gov: NASA, 10–11 (arm), 13; NASA's Goddard Space Flight Center, 22–23; pluto.jhuapl.edu: NASA/New Horizons Mission, 20–21; Science Source: Mikkel Juul Jensen, 14–15; Shutterstock: 3000ad, Cover; Dotted Yeti, 6, 12; Martin Nezval, 3, 24; Naeblys, 10–11 (ISS); Nerthuz, 10; NPeter, 7; olegbush, 1; tsuneomp, 4

Contents

CHAPTER 1

Working Far Away

It was November 26, 2018. A new robot was landing on Mars! Soon, scientists got a picture from it. It showed the planet's **surface**.

surface: the outside of an object

Space Jobs

Scientists use robots for many jobs. Some bots explore Mars. Other bots fly around planets. Some are big arms. They're like tools in space.

distance from Earth to Mars
more than 35 million miles (56 million kilometers)

PARTS OF A Mars Rover

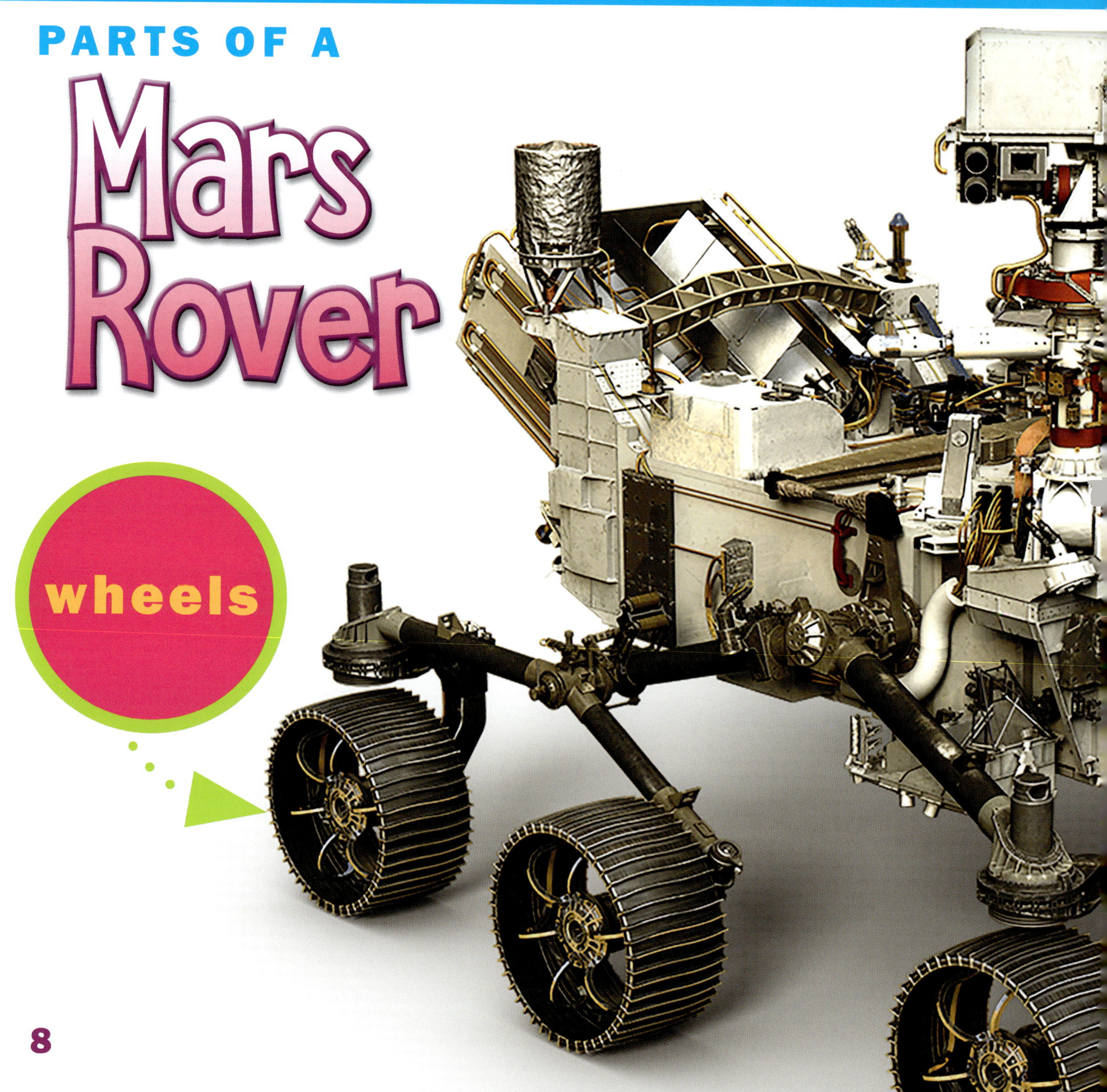

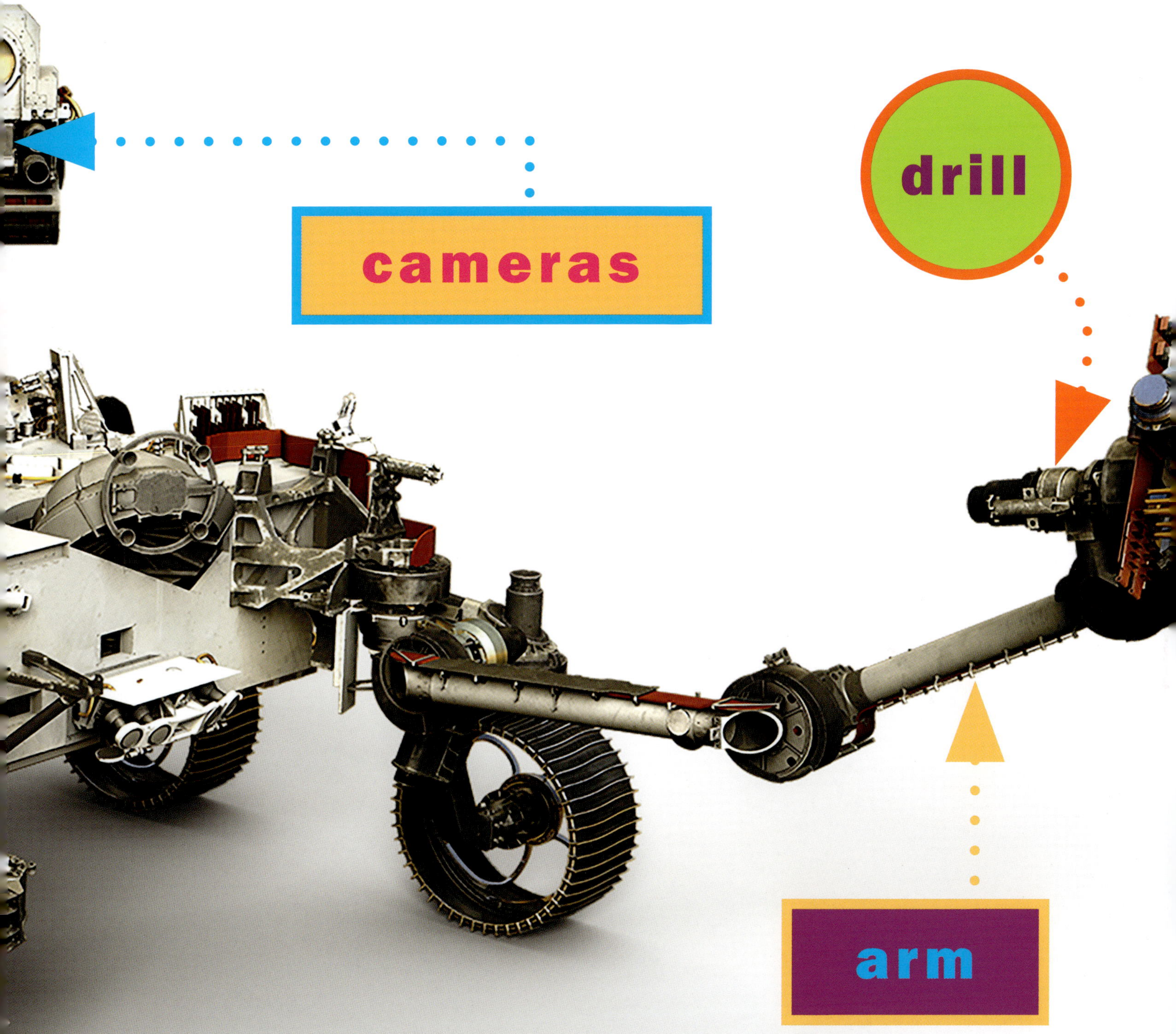

cameras

drill

arm

CHAPTER 2

In Space

The **space station** circles Earth. Arm bots sit outside the station. People use them to fix the building in space.

space station: a building in space where people can live

FACT
People on Earth move the station's arm bots.

Far Away

Scientists also send bots to planets and moons. Bots circle around them. They take pictures. They **measure** temperatures.

measure: to find out the size or amount of something

Bots in Space

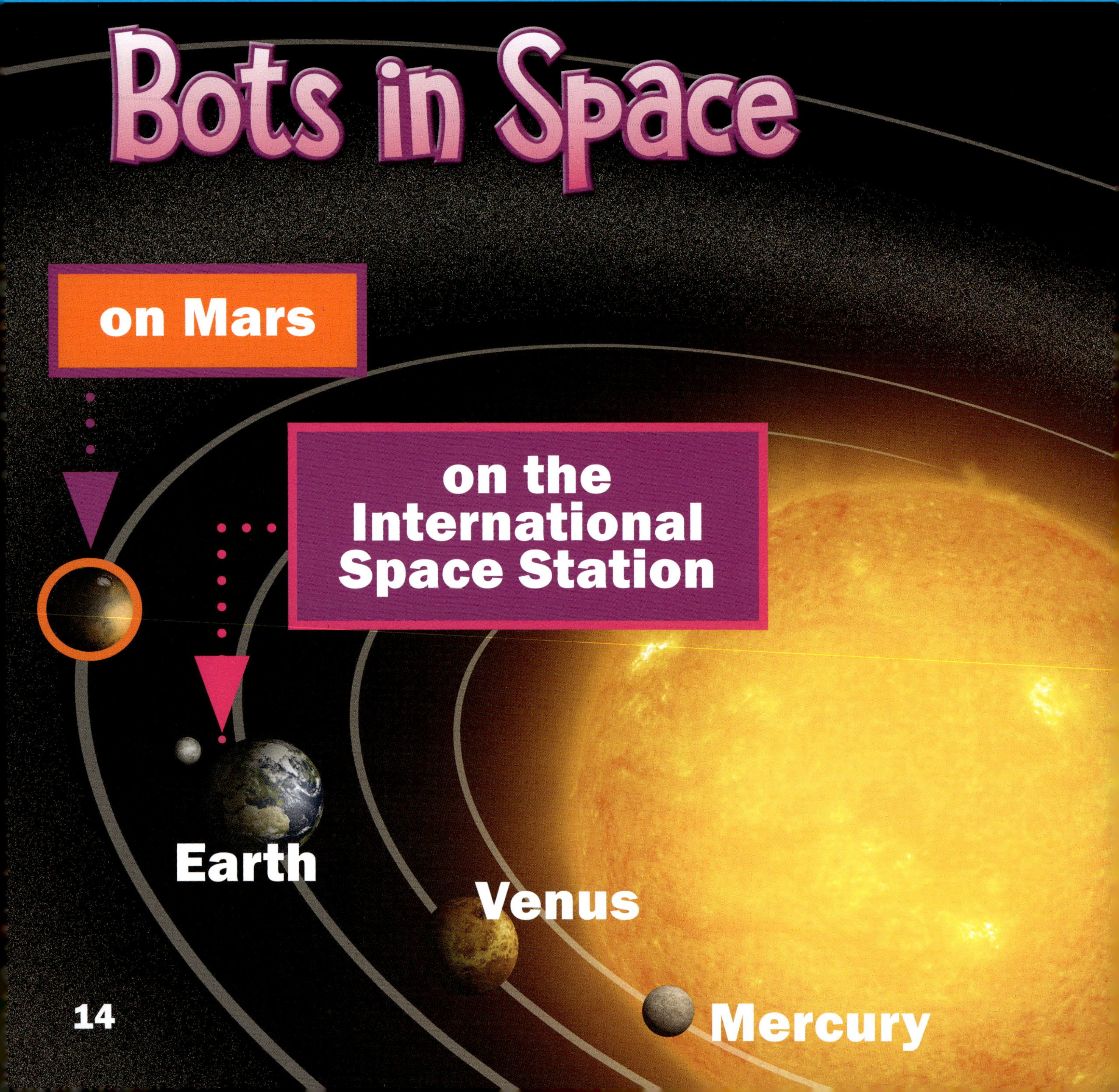

on Mars

on the International Space Station

Earth

Venus

Mercury

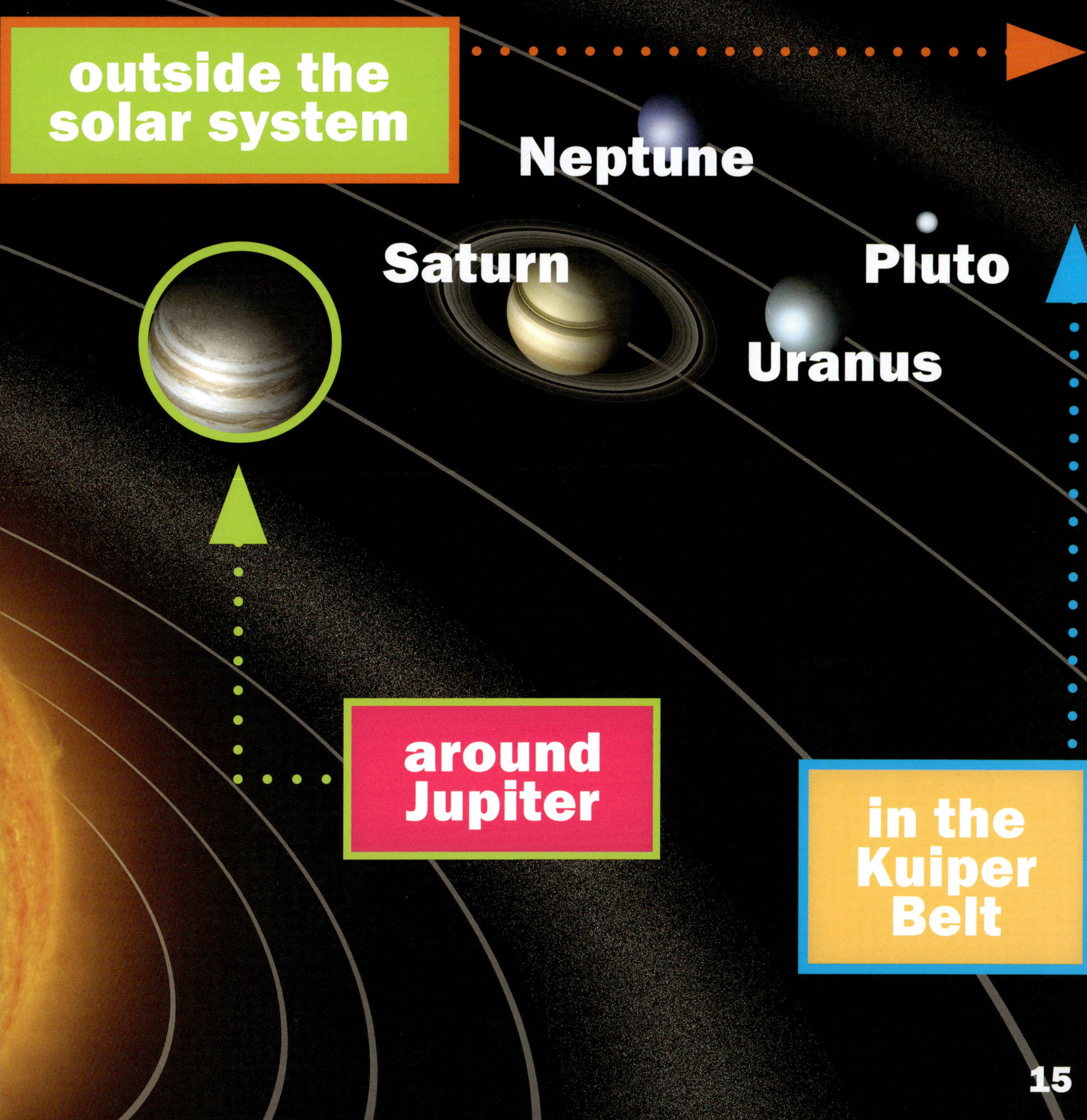
outside the solar system
Neptune
Saturn
Pluto
Uranus
around Jupiter
in the Kuiper Belt

CHAPTER 3

Landing

People can't get to Mars yet. But robots can. Curiosity has been there since 2012. It drills into the ground. It sends information back to Earth.

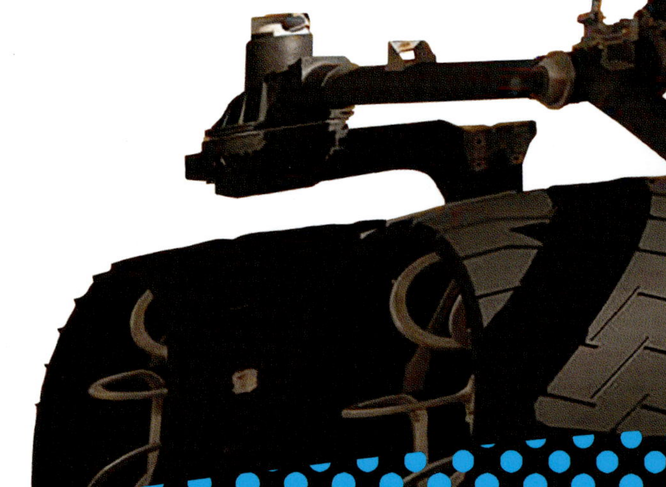

Learning in Space

In 2018, InSight landed on Mars. This bot can't move. But it has a long arm. This bot measures ground movement.

People wonder what's in space. Bots will help them find out.

The InSight Bot's Weight
794 pounds
(360 kilograms)

Bonus Facts

Bots have been to Pluto and Saturn.

The first bot went to **space** in 1957.

InSight's arm is about 6 feet (2 meters) long.

Two bots are outside the solar system.

solar system: the planets and space objects that circle the sun

READ MORE/WEBSITES

Clark, Neil. *Rusty the Squeaky Robot.* London: Words & Pictures, 2018.

Larson, Kirsten W. *Space Robots.* Robotics in Our World. Mankato, MN: Amicus High Interest/Amicus Ink, 2018.

Noll, Elizabeth. *Space Robots.* World of Robots. Minneapolis: Bellwether Media, Inc., 2018.

Robotics
kidsahead.com/subjects/1-robotics

Robotics: Facts
idahoptv.org/sciencetrek/topics/robots/facts.cfm

Robots for Kids
www.sciencekids.co.nz/robots.html

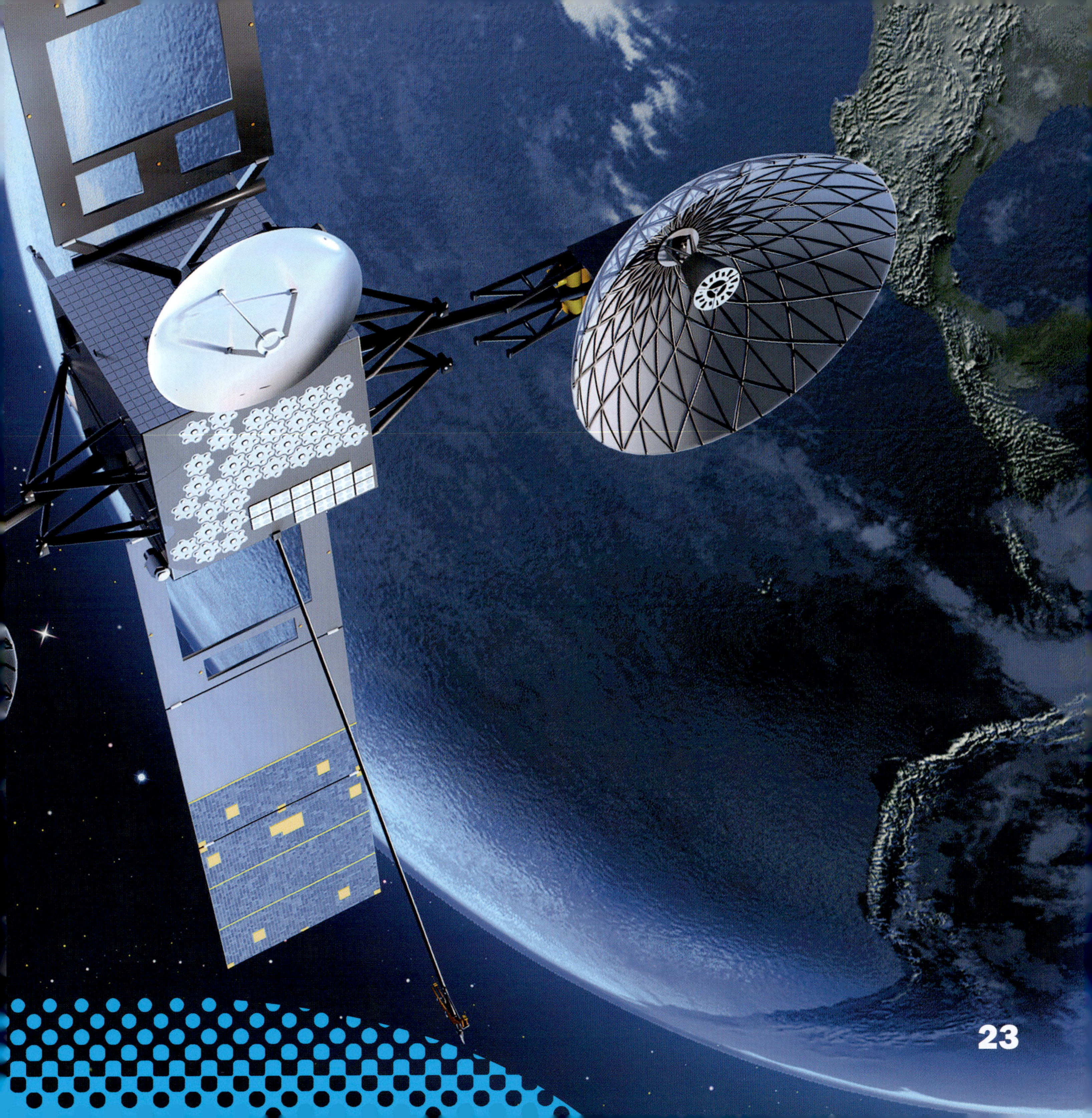

GLOSSARY

measure (MEH-zhur)—to find out the size or amount of something

solar system (SOH-luhr SYS-tum)—the planets and space objects that circle the sun

space station (SPAYS STAY-shun)—a building in space where people can live

surface (SUR-fus)—the outside of an object

INDEX